HOW TO PLAY MANDOLIN.

Jack Tottle.

HAL•LEONARD®

Also by the Author
Bluegrass Mandolin, Oak Publications

Exclusive distributors:

Hal Leonard
7777 West Bluemound Road
Milwaukee, WI 53213
Email: info@halleonard.com

Hal Leonard Europe Limited
42 Wigmore Street
Marylebone, London, W1U 2RN
Email: info@halleonardeurope.com

Hal Leonard Australia Pty. Ltd.
4 Lentara Court
Cheltenham, Victoria, 3192 Australia
Email: info@halleonard.com.au

Cover design by Pearce Marchbank
Photographs by David Gahr (page 41), Don Kissil (page 53), John Lee (page 8),
Herbert Wise (pages 15, 24, 34, 37), Phil Zimmerman (courtesy of Muleskinner News) (page 53).

Order No. AM35163
US International Standard Book Number: 0.8256.2354.5
UK International Standard Book Number: 0.7119.0450.2

Printed in the EU

Contents

To the Teacher

This book is designed to teach the fundamentals of mandolin technique through familiar tunes which are enjoyable to play.

There is considerable scope for flexibility. Newcomers to music as well as those with prior knowledge can begin playing these tunes right away, as they are written in both standard music notation and the simpler tablature. Chord symbols included with each piece encourage the student to play accompaniment as well as the melody. They also facilitate having the teacher or another student play guitar chords to accompany the mandolin. (Bringing a mandolin student and a guitar student together at the appropriate time can do wonders for the enthusiasm and musical understanding of each.)

Overall, the book provides a framework within which the teacher can employ his own individual style of instruction. (There is plenty of room in the margins for his personal notes to the student). The material presented is arranged so as to expedite this approach, while providing a carefully ordered—yet exciting—learning experience for the student.

To the Student

The mandolin is an old instrument which is at the same time quite modern. Both folk and classical music have been played on it for centuries in Europe. In America the mandolin has been used recently in many musical styles—from pop to ragtime—from country and bluegrass to blues and rock.

This small, easy-to-handle instrument has a bright sparkling sound. Whether or not you have a prior knowledge of music, you will find you can quickly learn to accompany songs on it and play melodies.

This book is designed to get you playing music you enjoy as soon as possible. It uses both standard music notation and a simplified system called tablature, which is clearly explained in the text.

You'll encounter very little in the way of memorizing musical terms or playing repetitious exercises. Nevertheless, as you go through the book, you will not only learn to play a number of excellent tunes, you'll also gain a firm understanding of the techniques involved. You'll then have both a solid repertoire of tunes you can play and the skills necessary to progress further.

Starting Out

Parts of the Mandolin

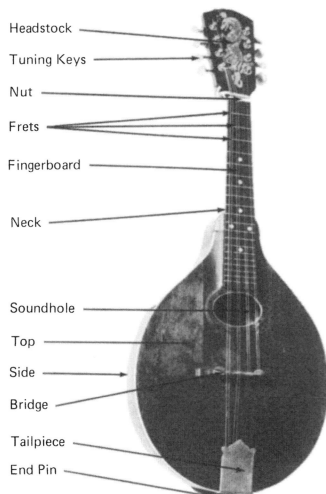

Headstock

Tuning Keys

Nut

Frets

Fingerboard

Neck

Soundhole

Top

Side

Bridge

Tailpiece

End Pin

Tuning

Before beginning, be sure your mandolin is in tune. Any music store should tune it for you without charge, and Appendix I in the back of the book shows you how to do it yourself.

Notice that the mandolin's eight strings are strung in pairs. Each pair consists of two strings tuned to the same note and is played as though it were just one string. The highest-pitched pair (that is, the thinnest) will be called simply the *first string*; the next pair, the *second string*, and so on.

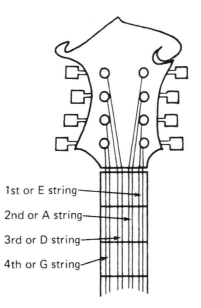

1st or E string

2nd or A string

3rd or D string

4th or G string

The Pick

There are many different pick styles available, and those shown in the picture are all fine for the mandolin. Many people find a large pick easier to hold comfortably, and a stiff pick generally gives the best tone.

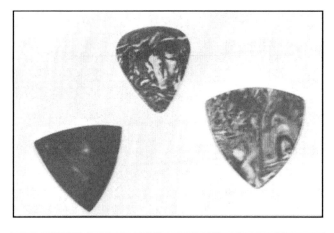

Holding The Mandolin

The mandolin is light and easy to hold, but you should use a strap, as shown. This allows your left hand to move freely over the fingerboard.

The strap also holds the mandolin *upright*, and parallel to your body. This lets your left hand press the strings against the fingerboard in a natural, comfortable manner.

The Brush Stroke

Hold the pick as shown in the picture, keeping your right hand as *relaxed* as you can. Play lightly across all four strings of the mandolin with a single downstroke.

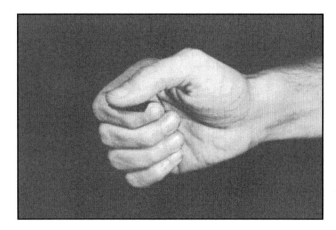

The brush stroke.

The motion should come from your *wrist*, not your arm; it's as though you were tapping a very small nail with a tiny hammer. Repeat the brush stroke until it feels comfortable.

The G Chord

Now, for a more musical sound . . .

(1) Begin by supporting the mandolin gently with your left hand. Press down the tip of your first (or index) finger just *behind* the second fret of the second string.

(2) Complete the chord by pressing the tip of your second (or middle) finger just behind the third fret of the first string. Be sure both fingers are holding the strings firmly against the frets.

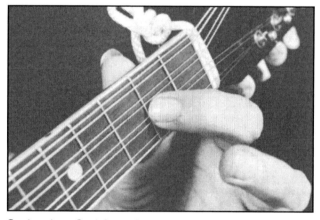

2nd string, 2nd fret—*b*

Notes played: g — d — b — g

G Chord

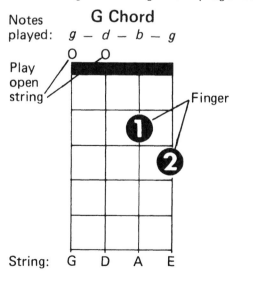

Play open string

Finger

String: G D A E

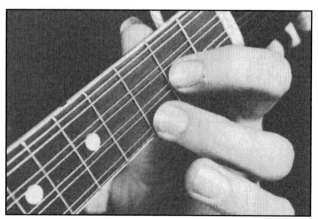

Complete G chord

(3) Play the brush stroke across all four strings as you did before. Repeat until you have a smooth, clean sound.

All four notes should blend into one full chord. If any string does not sound clear, make sure you're pressing tight enough. Adjust your fingers by moving closer to or farther from the frets if necessary. (Long fingernails can interfere with pressing down—cut them if they need it.)

Notice in the photo that all knuckles are bent and that the fingers pressing the strings come down almost perpendicularly to the fingerboard. This gives you the maximum force against the string with the least effort on your part.

Tablature

Tablature is a simplified form of writing music. Later sections of the book include tunes written in tablature as well as in standard music notation.

Here's how the G chord would look in tablature:

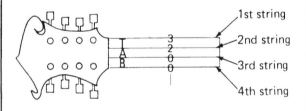

Each of the staff's four horizontal lines represents a string. The numbers show at which fret each string is noted.

In the example above, the second string is noted at the second fret and the first string at the third fret. The third and fourth strings are played open; O's are thus written on the third and fourth lines.

Larry Rice, ex-mandolin player with *J.D. Crowe & the New South.*

The C Chord

Once you can do a G chord the C chord isn't hard at all:

C Chord
(g — e — c — e)

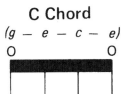

Play it several times using the brush stroke, as you did with G. Once you feel comfortable with C, try switching to the G chord and back to C again.

Now, play the brush stroke once in C, once in G, again, and so forth. This (C—G—C) is a basic chord progression for many songs. See how quickly you can move from one chord to the other, while still ensuring that each string comes out smooth and clear.

C chord written in tablature

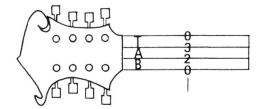

Playing in Rhythm

Good rhythm is just as important as playing your chords well.

Play your brush stroke with a G chord repeatedly. Keep a *very even* rhythm and count aloud:

One - two - three - four - One - two - three - four - *and so on.*

Then do the same with a C chord.

Next, try changing chords in rhythm. Use the same count, playing the G chord four times, the C four times, then back to G, and continue until the changes come easily:

G   C

One - two - three - four - One - two - three - four- *and so on.*

Keep your count slow enough so there is no interruption in the rhythm when you change chords.

Now you're ready to accompany a song:

C   G

Hush little ba – by   don't say a word, _____

G   C

Papa's gonna buy you a   mock – ing bird. _____ And

C   G

If that mock – ing   bird don't sing, _____

G   C

Papa's gonna buy you a   dia – mond ring. _____

Notice that you play the final beat of each line even though you don't sing on it.

The Single-String/Brush Accompaniment

For a more varied accompaniment you can pick individual strings and use brush strokes too.

Form a G chord with your left hand. Then:

(1) Play the fourth string (the thickest one).
(2) Play a brush stroke across all four strings.
(3) Play the third string.
(4) Play another brush stroke across all four strings.

In rhythm this will be:

| 4th | ↓ | 3rd | ↓ | 4th | ↓ | 3rd | ↓ |

One - two - three - four - One - two - three - four -

You can play a C chord accompaniment in exactly the same way.

Now let's try it in a song:

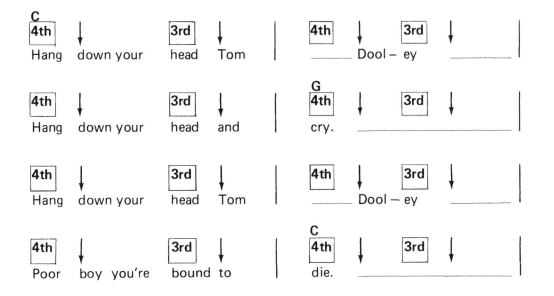

Some More Chords

Once you know a few chords you can accompany a great many songs. Some of the most useful are the following:

F

(c — f — a — f)

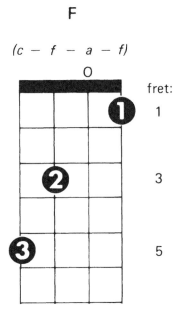

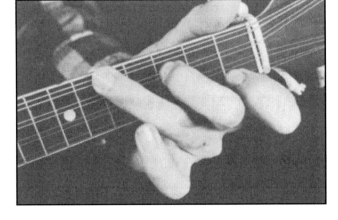

fret:
1

3

5

A

(c♯ —e — a — e)

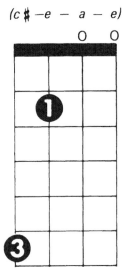

2

6

D

(a — d — a —f♯)

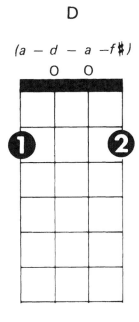

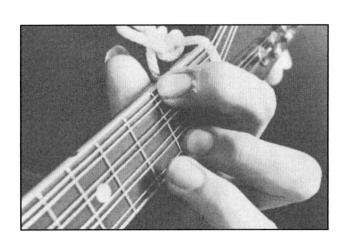

E7

(g♯ — d — b — e)

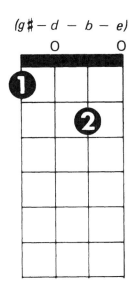

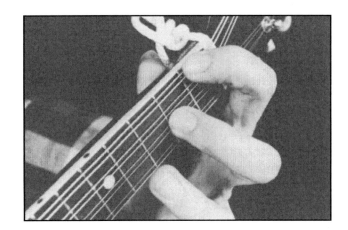

These chords will allow you to play the accompaniment for most of the songs in this book. When you do run into an unfamiliar chord, look it up in the chord dictionary in the back of the book (Appendix III).

Playing Melodies

Now that you can use basic chords, you're ready to start playing melodies using individual notes. Standard music notation (for those already familiar with it) and tablature are given in this chapter. Use whichever you prefer.

Press your third string down at the second fret. Play four evenly-spaced downstrokes, hitting your third string only:

Count aloud: One – two – three – four –

This would be written:

Standard Music Notation:

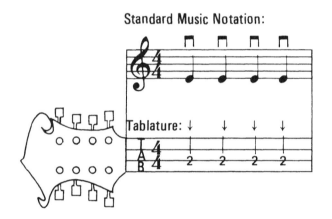

From the box on page 8 you already know why the tablature line appears this way—

(1) The numbers written on the 3rd line of the staff mean that the 3rd string is to be played.

(2) For each number *2*, the string is played once at the second fret.

Now, try playing the following phrase, using all downstrokes:

Standard Music Notation:

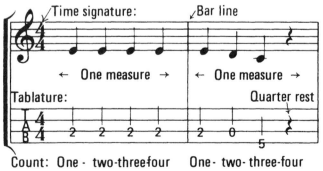

Count: One - two-threefour   One - two- three-four

Notice that in the second measure you play: third string, second fret—third string, open—fourth string, fifth fret. You don't play at all on the final beat, since a rest is indicated.

Left-Hand Fingering

It's important to use the correct finger whenever you play individual notes. Use the following rule unless otherwise indicated:

1st or 2nd fret:	First, or index, finger
3rd or 4th fret:	Second, or middle, finger
5th or 6th fret:	Third, or ring, finger
7th fret:	Fourth, or little, finger

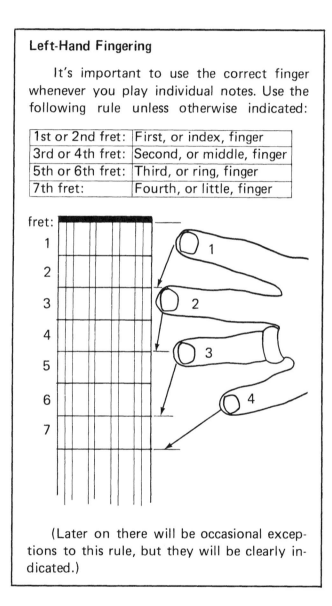

(Later on there will be occasional exceptions to this rule, but they will be clearly indicated.)

Now we'll play the melody for the first song you accompanied, "Hush Little Baby" (p. 10). Be sure to give the rests their full value. (You might say the word "rest" on each beat for which no note is played.)

Hush Little Baby

Arranged and adapted by Jack Tottle

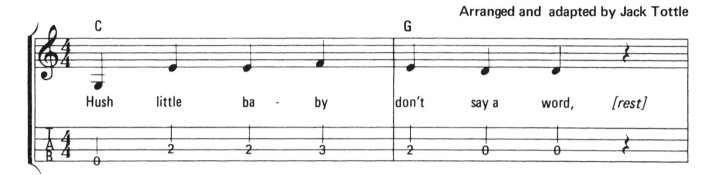

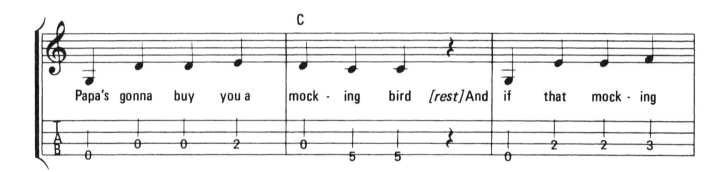

And if that diamond ring is glass,
Papa's gonna buy you a looking glass.
And if that looking glass gets broke,
Papa's gonna buy you a billy goat.

And if that billy goat don't pull,
Papa's gonna buy you a cart and bull.
And if that cart and bull fall down,
You'll still be the sweetest baby in town.

Note: The words are included just for reference and wouldn't normally be sung at the same time you play the melody. You can, however, sing the melody to the chord accompaniment you played earlier, and then play it solo on your mandolin between verses.

This melody can also be played an octave higher, giving you the additional brilliance of the mandolin's high strings.

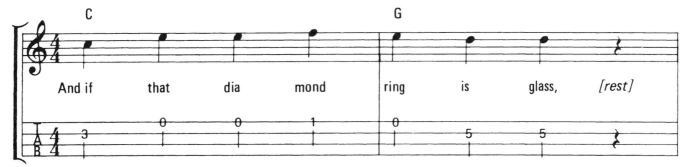

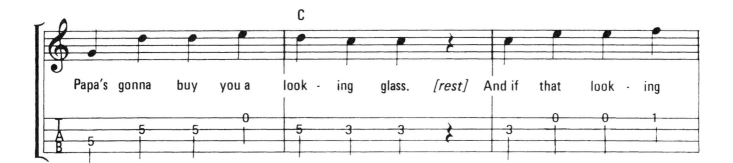

Let's try a favorite country guitar tune next. Notice that most of the measures have a quarter rest on the second beat.

Wildwood Flower

Arranged and adapted by Jack Tottle

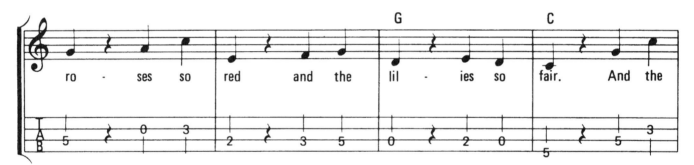

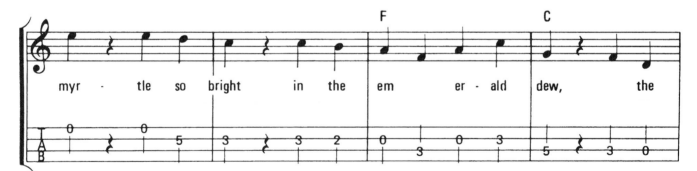

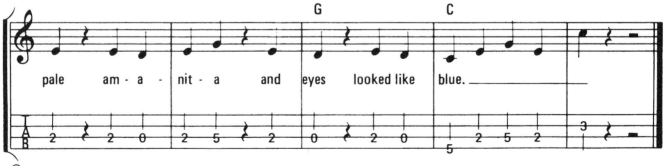

Using Down-Up Strokes

Start by playing the exercise you did on p. 14 again, doing the series of downstrokes in even rhythm:

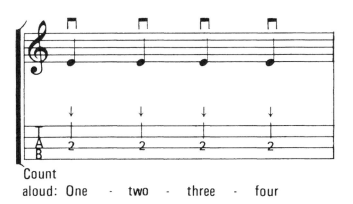

Count
aloud: One - two - three - four

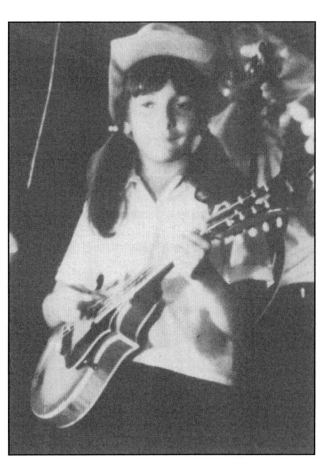

Now, tap your foot along. Your foot should hit the floor each time you count a beat.

Next, keep your foot tapping in the same rhythm and add an *upstroke* ("and") after each downstroke:

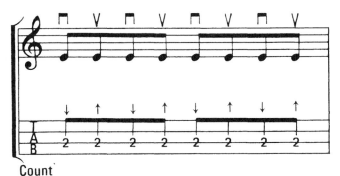

Count
aloud: One-and- two- and-three- and - four - and

Your foot (and pick) will still be moving down each time you count a beat. Both will then move back up each time you count "and."

These down-up strokes are called *eighth notes*. Notice that they look like quarter notes except that they are joined together by a horizontal beam.

Since two eighth notes take the same length of time as one quarter note, there can be eight eighth notes per measure in $\frac{4}{4}$ time.

Now let's play a simple phrase that will form the basis of our next tune, "Woody's Rag," by Woody Guthrie. Woody Guthrie was an important songwriter, singer and inspiration to many folk performers. He was also a mandolin player. Before learning this tune, let's play the simple phrase it's built around:

Use the correct left-hand fingering (second finger at third and fourth frets, and third finger at the fifth fret). Play the phrase several times without pausing, keeping the rhythm very steady.

Now try the same phrase moved over to the third and fourth strings:

And, again, the same thing on the first and second strings:

The end of the tune is just a little different. Keep your beat steady and remember that while a series of eighth notes is played as a series of down-up strokes, quarter notes are single down-strokes.

Once you can do these phrases, all you have to do in order to play the tune is put them together in the proper sequence.

Woody's Rag

Woody Guthrie

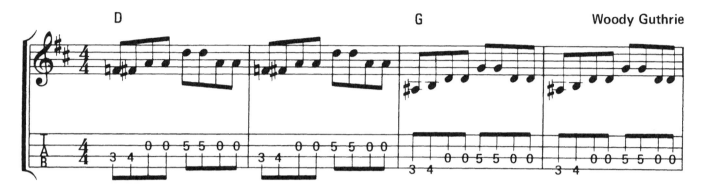

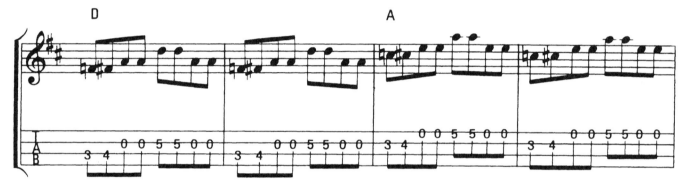

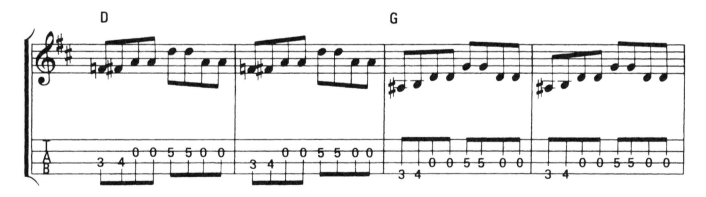

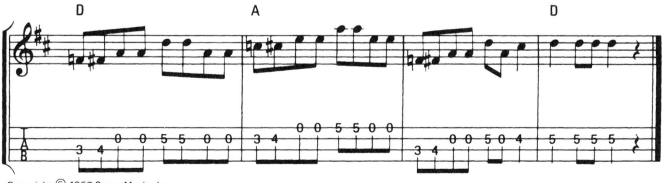

This next tune is a sea chanty; notice how the phrase in measure nine (*) leads into the following measure. This kind of passage, which does not directly correspond to the tune, is called a *run*. Runs are often used to fill in during pauses, or at the ends of verses or choruses.

Blow Ye Winds In The Morning

Arranged and adapted by Jack Tottle

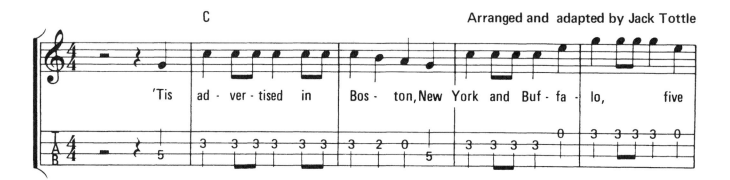

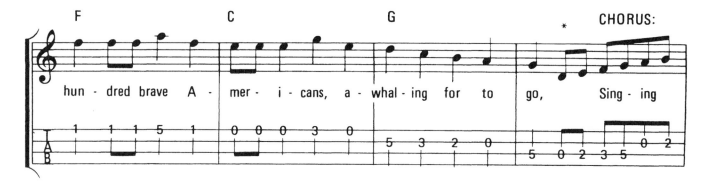

They'll send you to New Bedford,
That famous whaling port,
And give you to some land-sharks
To board and fit you out.

Chorus

They send you to a boarding house
There for a time to dwell.
The thieves there, they are thicker
Than the other side of hell!

Chorus

They tell you of the clipper-ships
A-going in and out,
And say you'll take five hundred sperm
Before you're six months out.

Chorus

And now we're out to sail my boys,
The wind begins to blow,
One half the watch is sick on deck
And the other half below.

Chorus

The skipper's on the quarter-deck
A-squinting at the sails,
When up aloft the lookout sights
A mighty school of whales.

Chorus

Now clear away the boats, my boys,
and after him we'll travel,
But if you get too near his fluke
He'll kick you to the devil.

Chorus

Now we've got him turned up
We'll tow him alongside,
And over with our blubber hooks
To rob him of his hide.

Chorus

¾ or Waltz Time

Certain songs have three beats per measure instead of four. These are said to be in $\frac{3}{4}$ or *waltz time*. A $\frac{3}{4}$ measure may consist of three quarter notes:

or of six eighth notes:

Each measure of $\frac{3}{4}$ can be accompanied by hitting a single string followed by two brush strokes.

Count: One – two – three–One – two – three –

Here's a pretty straightforward version of an old favorite. Notice that in measure fourteen the number in parentheses (3), indicates that you use your *third* finger on the fourth string, fourth fret.

On Top Of Old Smokey

Arranged and adapted by Jack Tottle

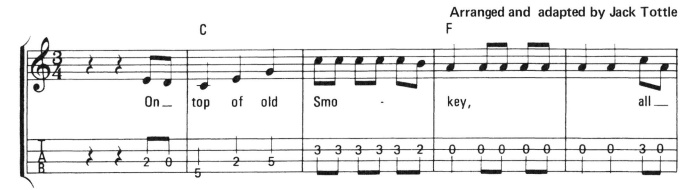

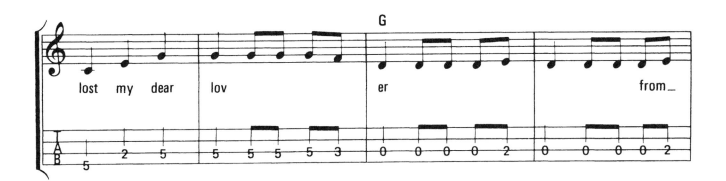

More verses on next page

For courting is pleasure, but parting is grief.
And a false-hearted true love is worse than a thief.

The thief he may rob you, and take all you save,
But a false-hearted true love will lead you to
    the grave.

As sure as the dew drop falls on the green corn
Last night he stayed with me, but today he is gone.

"When I Was Single" is another example of $\frac{3}{4}$ time. In keeping with the sentiments expressed, play it faster and lighter than the preceding song.

When I Was Single

Arranged and adapted by Jack Tottle

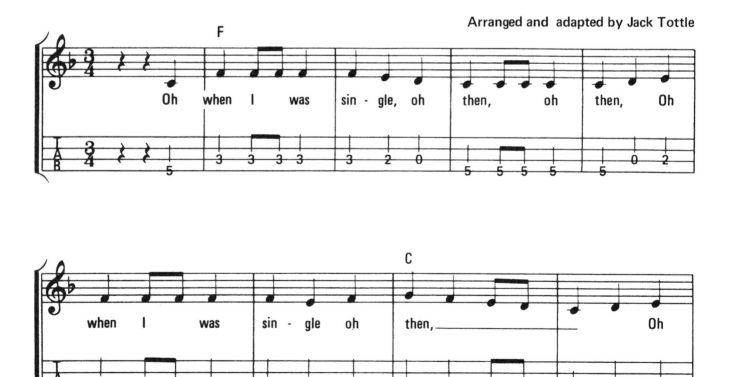

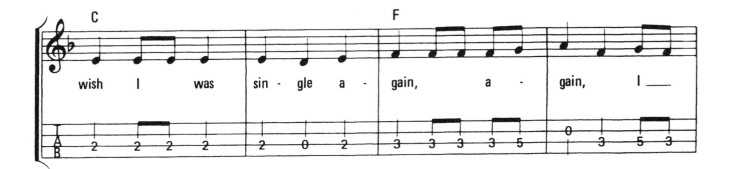

I married me a wife, oh then, oh then,
I married me a wife, oh then.
I married me a wife, she's the trial of my life,
And I wish I was single again, again,
I wish I was single again.

My wife she died, oh then, oh then,
My wife she died, oh then,
My wife she died and I laughed till I cried
To think I was single again, again,
To think I was single again.

I married me another, oh then, oh then,
I married me another, oh then.
I married me another, she's the devil's
    stepmother,
And I wish I was single again, again,
I wish I was single again.

The Slide

The slide is a way of producing two notes with just one stroke of the pick, by sliding a finger of the left hand.

Use your third finger to hold down the second string, fourth fret. Play a single downstroke and immediately slide your finger up to the fifth fret. Press the string firmly against the fingerboard as you slide, to produce the cleanest sound possible.

Slide—*c♯* to *d*. Position before slide.

After slide—third finger on fifth fret.

The symbol ⓢ indicates a slide in tablature:

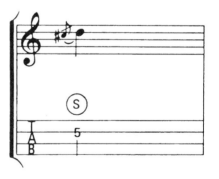

Notice that the slide begins one fret *below* the note shown. The final note of the slide falls squarely on the beat, with the previous note heard just an instant before.

In this next song each slide leads into a series of eighth notes; it's important to keep the timing even. Play measures one and three by themselves first without the slide, to hear the correct timing. Then add the slide, taking care not to alter the timing.

Red Apple Juice

Arranged and adapted by Jack Tottle

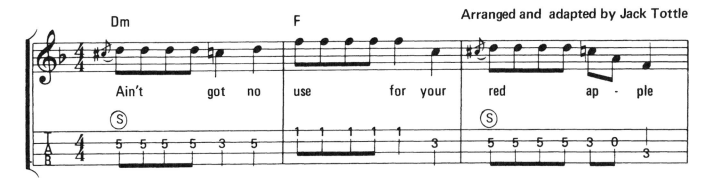

Ain't got no use for your red ap - ple

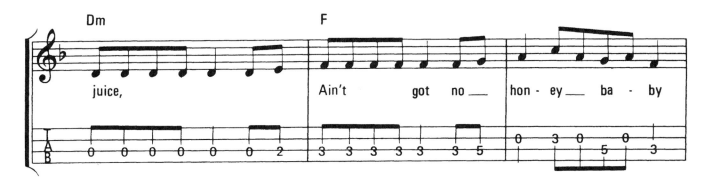

juice, Ain't got no ___ hon - ey ___ ba - by

now, Lord, Lord, Ain't got no ___

hon - ey ___ ba - by now.

More verses on next page

It's all I can do, and all I can say,
Can't keep on this a-way, Lord, Lord,
Can't keep on this a-way.

Who'll rock the cradle, who'll sing the song,
Who'll rock the cradle when I'm gone, Lord, Lord,
Who'll rock the cradle when I'm gone?

I'll rock the cradle, I'll sing the song,
I'll have another honey when you're gone, Lord,
    Lord,
I'll have another honey when you're gone.

"New River Train" is a fun one to play fast. Learn it at a comfortably slow tempo; when you can play it easily and very cleanly at this speed, try it a little faster. If it still sounds even and clear, try it still more rapidly. Don't, however, play so fast that some notes become muffled or the song speeds up or slows down in places.

New River Train

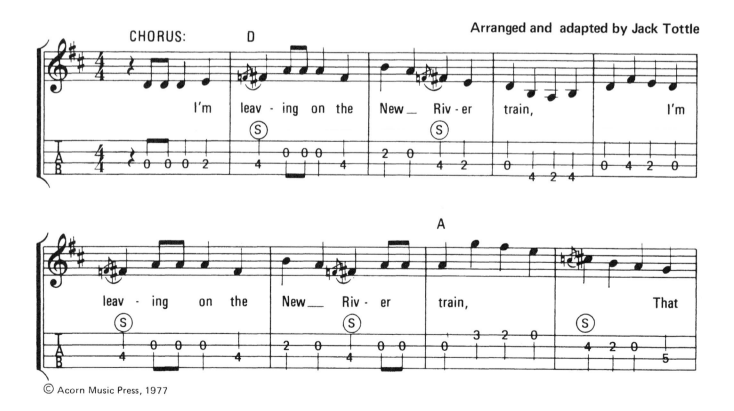

Arranged and adapted by Jack Tottle

Now darling, you can't love one, *(twice)*
You can't love one and still have your fun,
No, darling, you can't love one.

Darling, you can't love two, *(twice)*
You can't love two and think I'll be true,
No, darling, you can't love two.

Darling, you can't love three, *(twice)*
You can't love three and still be loving me,
No, darling, you can't love three.

Darling, now remember what you said, *(twice)*
You know you said you'd sooner see me dead
Than leaving on that New River train.

Here's a mountain square dance tune. Play it at
a medium tempo, but with plenty of life.

Cindy

Arranged and adapted by Jack Tottle

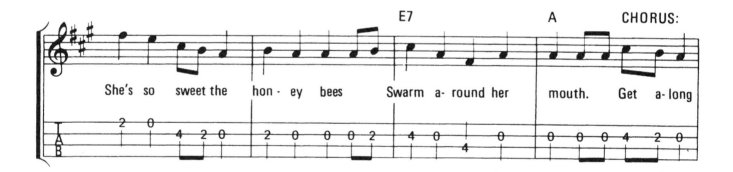

Cindy in the springtime,
Cindy in the fall,
If I don't get that pretty little gal
I won't have none at all.

Chorus

I wish I was an apple
Hanging on a tree,
And every time that Cindy passed
She'd take a bite of me.

Chorus

Cindy got religion,
She hollered all around,
She got so full of glory
She shook her stockings down.

Chorus

Cindy got religion,
She had it once before,
But when she hears that fiddle
She's the first one on the floor.

Double String Melodies

Although the tunes up until now have all been played on single strings, it is possible to play using double strings as well. This allows you to play the melody on one string and, at the same time, a harmony part on another.

First, try a downstroke on your highest two strings (that is, the first and second strings). Make sure that your attack is sharp enough so that both strings sound at the same instant. Repeat the downstroke until it sounds smooth and clean. Then try it on the other pairs of strings.

Next, try the following exercise a few times. Keep your rhythm even, and your notes clean-sounding.

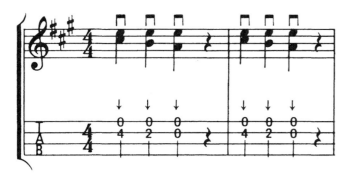

Jethro Burns, country and jazz mandolinist formerly of *Homer & Jethro*.

When the downstroke sounds good, try the down-up stroke, again on your first two strings. The idea is to get the upstroke to sound identical to the downstroke. Hold the pick loose, and be sure the first string doesn't sound any louder than the second.

After you feel comfortable with the open strings, see how smoothly you can play the following:

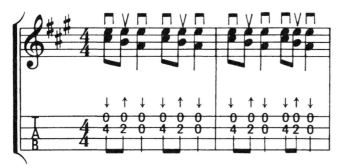

Now try this medium tempo dance tune. When you come to the end, return to the beginning without a pause and play it through again. (The melody here is in the lower part; this is generally true of double-string mandolin tunes.)

Boil Em Cabbage Down

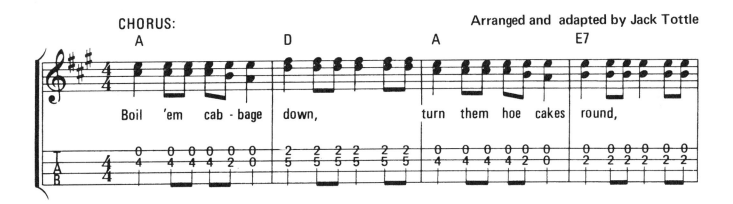

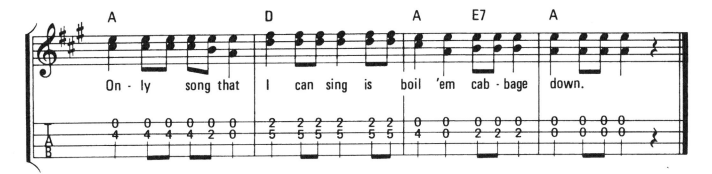

I went up on the mountain, give my horn a blow,
Thought I heard my darlin' say, "Yonder comes
my beau."

Hardest work I ever done was plowin' round a pine,
Easiest work I ever done was huggin' that gal of
mine.

Your hand is moved up the neck at the beginning of the next song. The numbers in parentheses above the tablature line show that your fourth finger plays the eighth fret; your second finger plays the fifth fret, etc.

Notice that in the seventh measure you return to normal fingering. The solo is short, so you may want to play it through at least twice in a row each time you do it.

(Note for those reading standard music notation: Roman numerals above a note indicate on which string that note is played when the left hand is moved up the neck.)

Give Me That Old Time Religion

Arranged and adapted by Jack Tottle

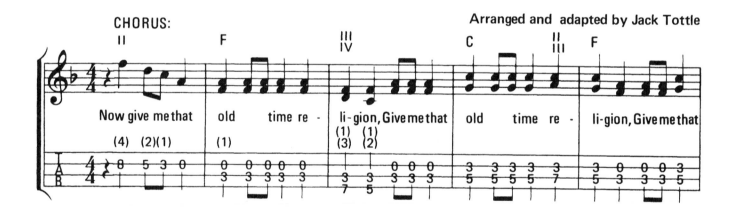

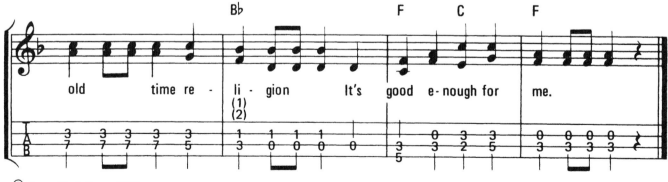

It was good for Paul and Silas, *(three times)*
And it's good enough for me.

It was good for our fathers, *(three times)*
And it's good enough for me.

It was good for our mothers, *(three times)*
And it's good enough for me.

Makes me shout when I get happy, *(three times)*
And it's good enough for me.

Makes me love everybody, *(three times)*
And it's good enough for me.

Mick Maloney

Mixed Single and Double Strings

Single and double-string playing can be interspersed within a song in a variety of ways, as the following tunes show. Lighten your touch a little when you come to double-string passages. This will keep the single-string parts from sounding weak by comparison.

In this next tune, the main melody notes are played on double strings, while the fill-in notes are played singly. Double strings are used to strengthen the ending.

Measure fifteen is in $\frac{2}{4}$ time, as shown by the new time signature, which just means it contains two beats instead of four, in this case two quarter notes.

Deep Blue Sea

Arranged and adapted by Jack Tottle

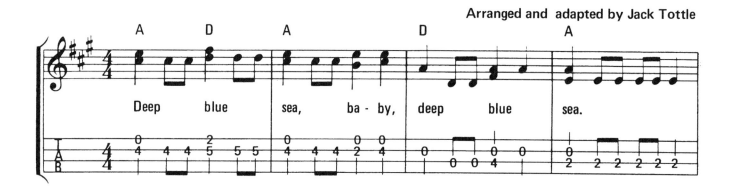

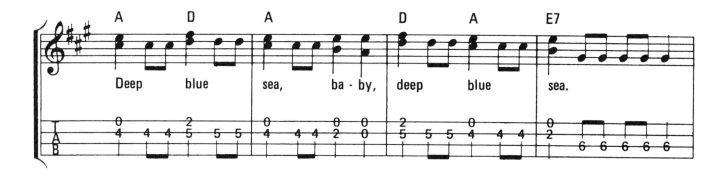

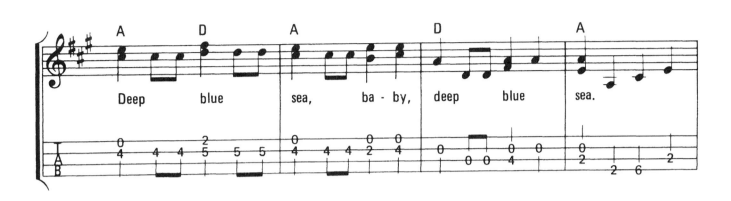

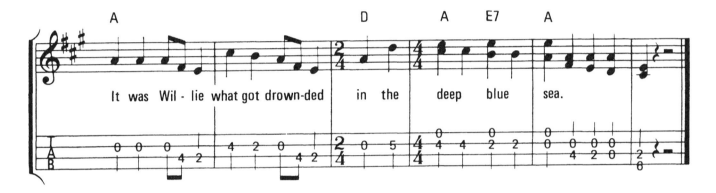

Dig his grave with a silver spade, *(three times)*
It was Willie what got drownded in the deep blue
    sea.

Lower him down with a golden chain, *(three times)*
It was Willie what got drownded in the deep blue
    sea.

Wrap him up in a silken shroud, *(three times)*
It was Willie what got drownded in the deep blue
    sea.

Start the slides in this next song, "Black-Eyed
Susie," at the *fifth* fret (with your third finger) and
move to the seventh fret. The fingering in parentheses indicates when to shift your hand.

Black Eyed Susie

Arranged and adapted by Jack Tottle

Black - eyed Su - sie come to town __ and all she wore was a

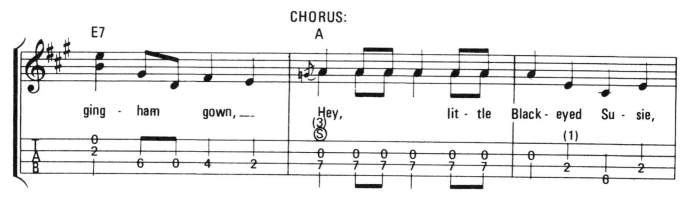

ging - ham gown, __ Hey, lit - tle Black - eyed Su - sie,

CHORUS:

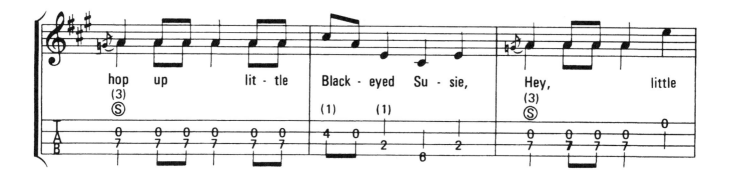

hop up lit - tle Black - eyed Su - sie, Hey, little

Black - eyed Su - sie, hey.

Black-eyed Susie, 'bout half grown,
Jumps on a man like a dog on a bone,

Chorus:
Hey, little black-eyed Susie,
Hop up, little black-eyed Susie,
Hey, little black-eyed Susie, hey.

Through the woods and 'cross the water
Some old man's gonna lose his daughter,

Chorus

Some get drunk and some get boozy,
I'll go home with black-eyed Susie,

Chorus

Bill Monroe, "Father of Bluegrass."

More Songs

By now you have a good grasp of basic mandolin technique. You have learned right- and left-hand techniques, can play single or double strings, and can do slides and shift up the neck. In this section you can use what you now know on some additional songs of various types.

Bill Bailey Won't You Please Come Home

Although the phrase in measures two and three may sound a little odd to you at first while you are playing it slowly, it should sound fine after you get it up to speed. Toward the end, the mandolin part gets a bit fancier than the actual melody of the song, which makes for an exciting finish. Watch for correct pick direction in the next-to-last measure.

Arranged and adapted by Jack Tottle

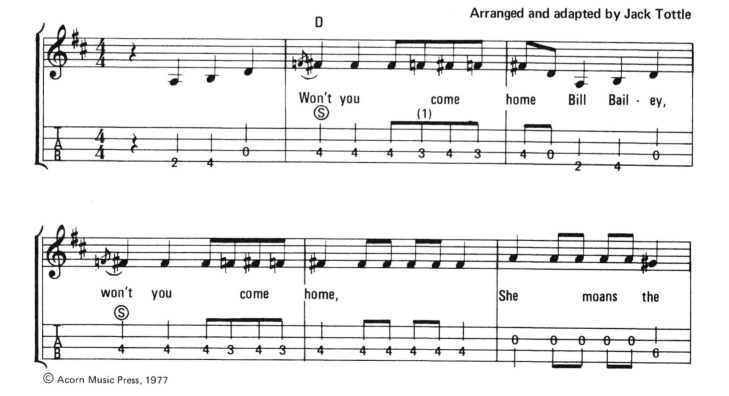

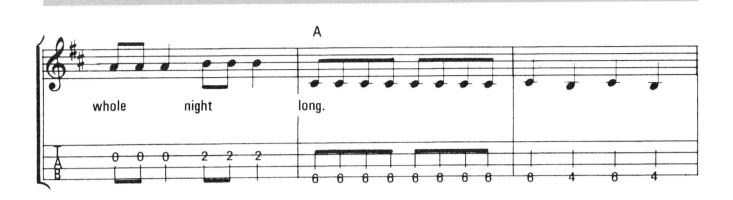

whole   night   long.

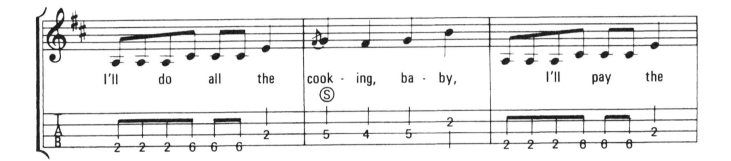

I'll   do   all   the   cook - ing, ba - by,   I'll   pay   the

rent,   I know   I've   done   you

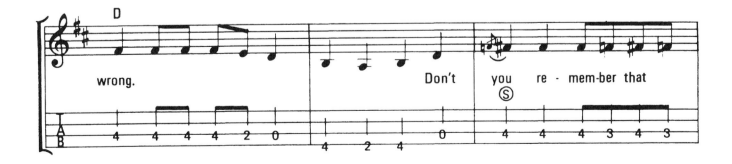

wrong.   Don't   you   re - mem-ber that

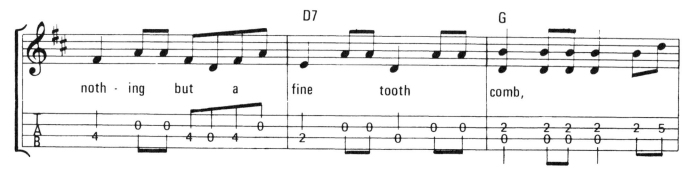

Lonesome Fugitive

This is a modern country song recorded by Merle Haggard. In the second and fourth lines of the chorus, the mandolin part shifts to a higher range than the actual melody of the song.

Liz and Casey Anderson

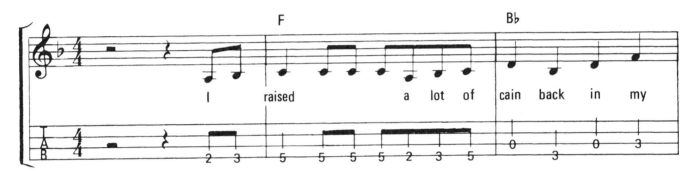

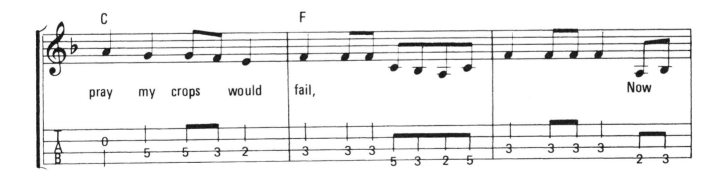

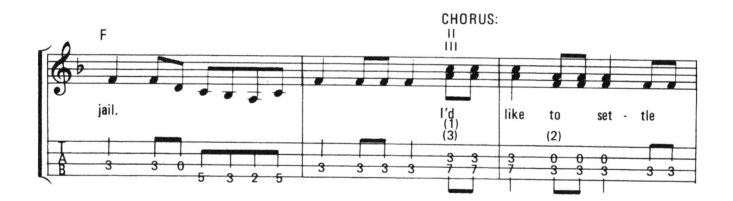

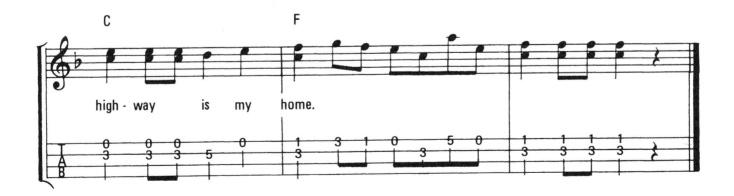

Rocky Top

A long-standing bluegrass favorite, this song should be performed about as fast as you can *comfortably* play, without sacrificing perfectly even timing and smooth picking.

Boudleaux and Felice Bryant

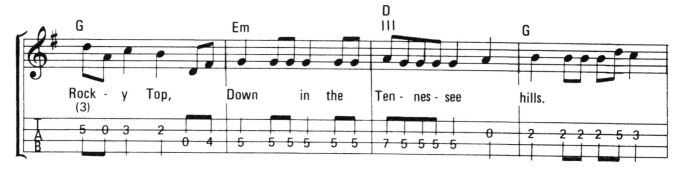

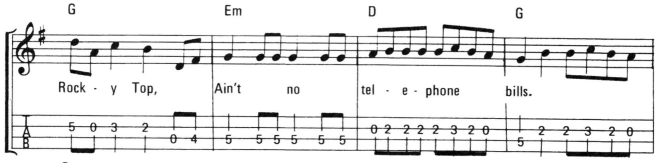

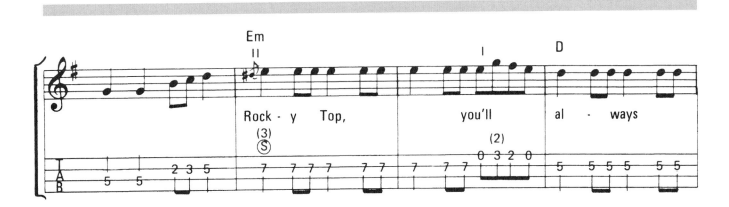

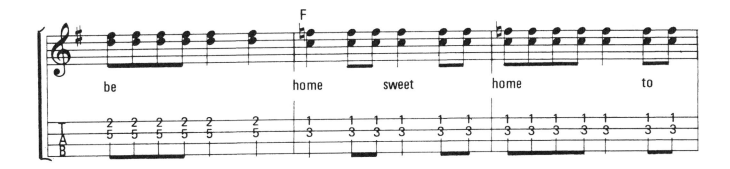

"Make Me A Pallet On Your Floor" is another well-known folk song. Played slowly, it can sound like a blues; played up-tempo it has a bluegrass feel.

Note: The D#⁰ chord (D sharp diminished) may be played:

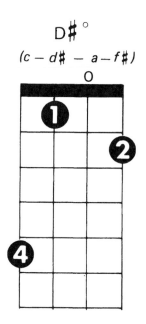

Make Me A Pallet On Your Floor

Arranged and adapted by Jack Tottle

Now won't you make me a pal - let on your floor,

make me a pal - let on your floor? Make it

long, make it low so no one will ev - er know,

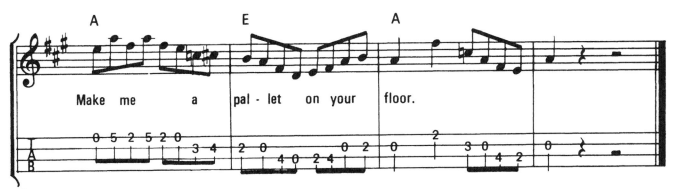

Make me a pal - let on your floor.

Mama Don't Allow

Here's a great song to play with other people, as it gives any number of instruments a chance to be spotlighted. Notice how the third finger slides to the seventh fret at the start.

Arranged and adapted by Jack Tottle

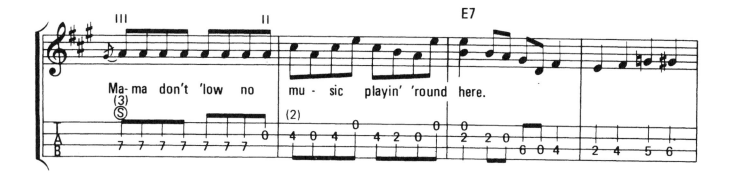

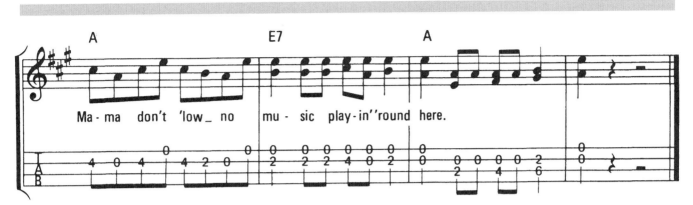

Ma - ma don't 'low _ no   mu - sic play - in' 'round here.

Mama don't 'low no mandolin playin' round here,
Mama don't 'low no mandolin playin' round here,
We don't care what mama don't 'low,
Gonna play that mandolin anyhow,
Mama don't 'low no mandolin playin' round here.

*Try putting these other instruments in place of
mandolin to make new verses:*

Mama don't 'low no guitar playin' round here . . .

Mama don't 'low no fiddle playin' round here . . .

Mama don't 'low no piano playin' round here . . .

Mama don't 'low no harmonizin' round here . . .

Frank Wakefield (*left*) and David Grisman.

Walk Right In

This song was a hit on the twelve-string guitar, but it works well on the mandolin, too. The finger work in the next-to-last measure is just a little tricky, so practice it separately a few times before you try the full song.

Words and music by Gus Cannon and H. Wood
Arranged by Erik Darling and Willard Svance

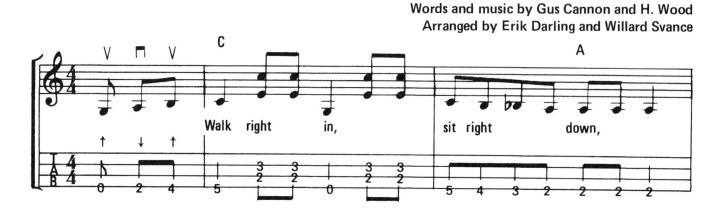

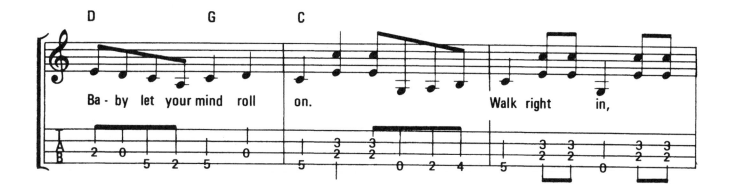

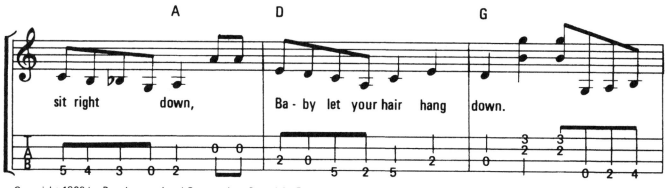

I'm Looking Through You

Beatles tunes work well on the mandolin, too. Notice the triple string parts in measures two, six and fourteen. For each three-note chord, try a slow brush with your pick across the strings, so that each note comes just an instant after the preceding one. The result is a ringing, harplike sound.

Verse

Lennon/McCartney

I'm look- ing through you, Where did you go? I thought I

knew you, What did I know? You don't look

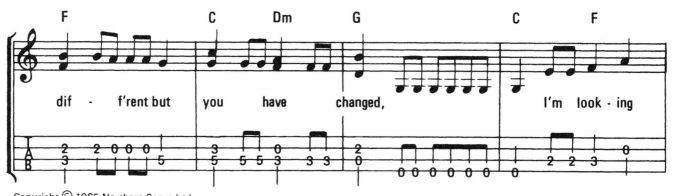

dif - f'rent but you have changed, I'm look - ing

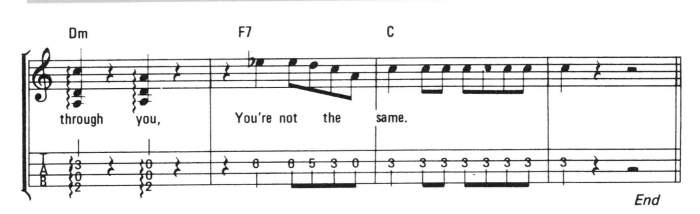

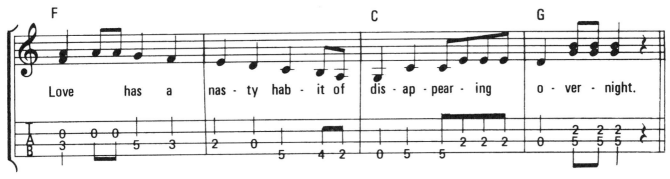

End by Repeating Verse

The next tune, ''Get Back,'' is another Beatles song that lends itself to the mandolin. On this one, you can get a syncopated feel by letting the last note of measure eight ring as you continue with even down-up strokes into the next measure.

Get Back

Lennon/McCartney

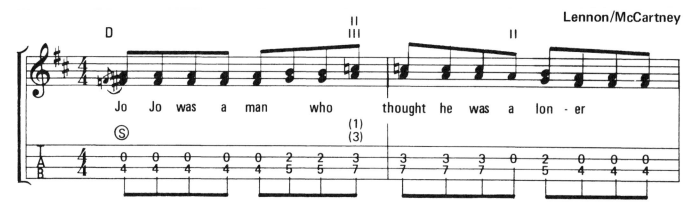

Jo Jo was a man who thought he was a lon - er

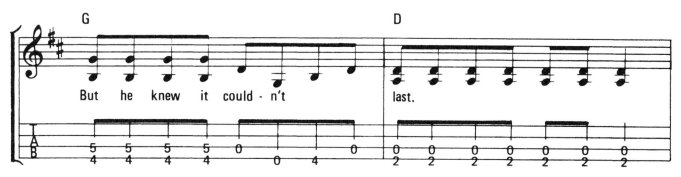

But he knew it could - n't last.

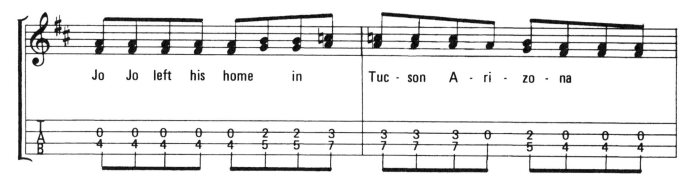

Jo Jo left his home in Tuc - son A - ri - zo - na

CHORUS:

for some Cal - i - for - nia grass. Get back!

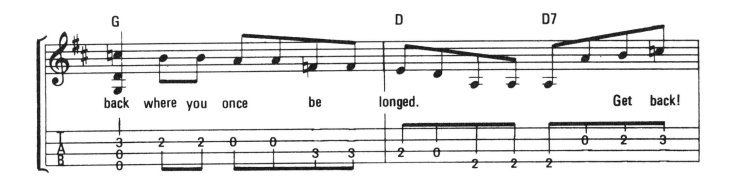

Appendices

I. Tuning

To tune the mandolin, you tighten or loosen the strings by adjusting the tuning keys. Tightening the string produces a higher note; loosening it makes the note lower.

Tuning from a pitch pipe:

Most music stores sell an item called a *pitch pipe*. The mandolin pitch pipe consists of four pipes mounted together. Blowing on the various pipes produces the four different notes to which the mandolin's strings are tuned.

Tuning from a piano:

A piano which is in good tune will provide a still more accurate reference for tuning. The notes on the piano keyboard which correspond to the mandolin's strings are shown below:

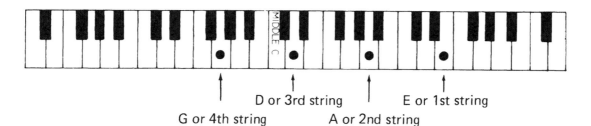

D or 3rd string   E or 1st string

G or 4th string   A or 2nd string

Tuning the mandolin to itself:

If the mandolin has gotten slightly out of tune, you can readiliy put it back in tune just by checking the strings against each other.

Each of the three upper open strings is tuned to the same note as the next *lower* string (lower in pitch) when pressed at the seventh fret:

Tuning from a tuning fork:

Another very accurate and easily portable reference for tuning is the *tuning fork*. The A (440 cycles per second) tuning fork is available at most music stores. It corresponds to the second string. Once the second string is in tune, the remaining strings can be tuned as just described.

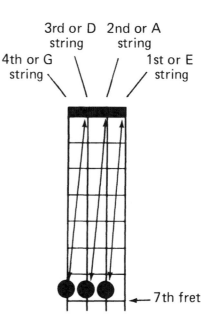

3rd or D   2nd or A
string   string

4th or G   1st or E
string   string

← 7th fret

II. Standard Music Notation on the Mandolin

If you already read music and wish to apply your knowledge to the mandolin, the following should be of help. Here are the notes corresponding to the open strings:

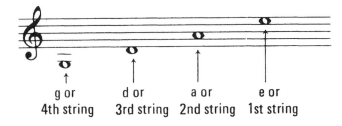

g or	d or	a or	e or
4th string	3rd string	2nd string	1st string

Each fret is one half-step from the next fret. The notes on the fourth string are as follows:

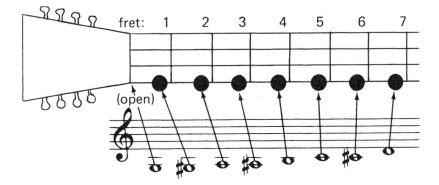

The same pattern holds for the other strings as well.

III. Chord Dictionary

The following diagrams show major, minor and seventh chords. The small circles (O) over certain strings indicate that they are played open. The numbers on the diagram indicate which fingers are used.

Some chords (A7, for example) show two strings held at the same fret by one finger. As shown in the next pictures, you have to flatten the knuckle to permit this. Holding two strings in this way is called a *barre*.

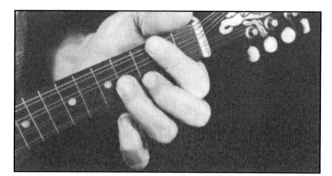

A7—Barre form

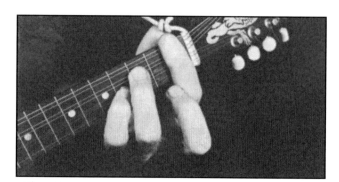

C# —Barre form

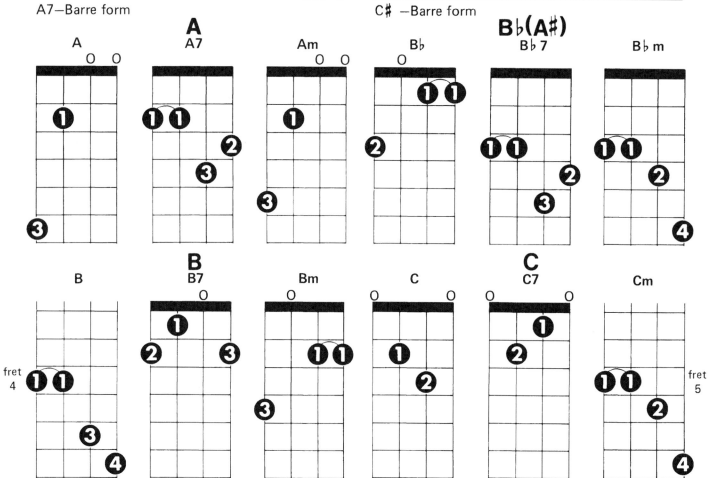

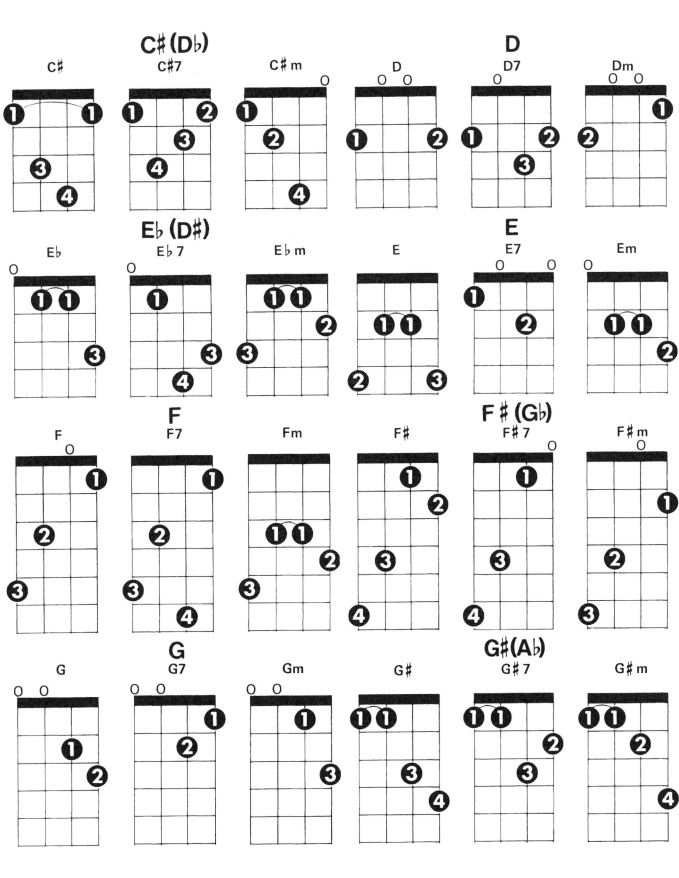